Jan…

The Curious Tale of Hare and Hedgehog

Andersen Press

One day Hare decided he would like to win something, so he went to see Hedgehog. Hedgehog lived in the little thatched cottage among those trees, under that little cloud. The cloud up in the sky where the birds are flying.

"Come on, let's have a race!" said Hare. "I wonder who will win!"

Of course, he thought he would win. Hare, that is.
Hare with his long legs.
But Hedgehog was lying on a rug on the grass behind his house, with his teapot beside him. He had just drunk a nice cup of tea and eaten a nice piece of cake, and he was smoking his pipe. He had a good book to read too.

"All right," said Hedgehog. "You start if you like. I'll just pop home for my running shoes and my wife, and then the race won't seem such a long way to me. Me with my short legs."

Well, Hare shot off at once! After all, he thought, getting a little start in a race never did any harm. Now he'd win even more easily!

Hare with his long legs.

Off ran Hare, fast as the wind, in the direction of Land's End.

He hadn't gone far before he caught up with Mr Jones the engine driver on his bike.
"Where are you off to so fast?" asked Mr Jones.
"Land's End," said Hare.
"I'll give you a lift if you like," said Mr Jones. "The train leaves at six-fifteen from Platform . . . ."

But Hare was out of hearing. Hare was haring along.
When he reached Land's End he thought he might as well get a little more of a start, and then he'd be even more of a winner.
Hare with his long legs.
So he ran on, in the direction of London Town.

On his way to London Town he passed the Mill of Dee, and there he met Billy the little dog and Kit Cat with her fiddle.
"Hey, why are you running like that, Hare?" asked Kit. "You with your long legs?"
"It's a race!" panted Hare. "A race with Hedgehog. I'm winning!"

"Wow! Real hairy," said Kit. "Never mind winning, come along with us! We're going to John o' Coats."
"Groats," said Billy. "John o' Groats."
"John o' Goats," said Kit—but Hare was off again already.

Careful, Hare, you with your long legs! London Town is a very busy place. Don't you know you mustn't cross the road when the lights are red? That was a close shave! If the kind old lady hadn't helped Hare over the road, he would probably have been squashed flat.

So Hare ran on, he ran out of London Town, and he thought he would go to Banbury Cross, because if he could get a little bit more of a start he would be even more of a winner.
Hare with his long legs.

Out in the open country again, he met Mr Greenwood the gamekeeper.
"And where are you off to so fast, young fellow?" asked the gamekeeper.
"It's a race!" panted Hare. "A race with Hedgehog. I'm winning!"
"No call for that," said the gamekeeper. "Who cares who wins?"

But Hare was off again, Hare with his long legs. And all of a sudden, snap! He had run right into Dodger the poacher's rabbit trap. One iron ring snapped shut around his forepaw and another iron ring around his hind leg.
The end of the race. The finish. All over and done with and not a hope in sight.

But then along came a runner. Maybe the runner could set Hare free?
"Who are you racing?" Hare asked the runner.
"I'm not racing anyone," said the runner. "Just running."
"How stupid!" said Hare. "I'd never do a thing like that!"

Then he remembered he'd been going to ask about the trap.
But by now the runner was out of sight.
Oh dear! What a terrible thing! Still no hope in sight, and Hare was afraid he'd see Hedgehog catching up any minute.

However, then the old man who lived in the woods came along and set Hare free. He bandaged his leg, and he didn't ask where Hare was going, or where he came from, he just wished him luck, and Hare limped on again at once.
Hare with his lame legs.
The reason the old man did not have to ask any questions was probably that he already knew the answers.

So Hare limped on and on along the road.
Cars and motorbikes and goodness knows
what else rushed by him.
He was afraid Hedgehog might catch up
with him and win after all—that was what
kept him going.

Now that his leg was bandaged up, Hare
wasn't as fast as he used to be.
Hare with his long legs.

But Hedgehog wasn't running the race at all.
When he rose to his feet, he had picked up his rug, his teapot and his teacup, and then he went home. Not very fast.
Hedgehog with his short legs.
He had not gone ten paces before he forgot all about the race.

His wife was in her rocking chair in the garden, having a little nap.
She had been knitting, and what with her knitting, she'd forgotten to cook a meal.
She hadn't even made any sandwiches.
Never mind.

“Fry us some eggs, will you, Hedgehog dear?” she said. “Two for you and two for me.”
So Hedgehog broke four eggs into the frying pan. Two for him and two for Mrs Hedgehog.

The Hedgehogs had a lovely house.
"Let's pack up a picnic and go out for the day," said Hedgehog.
"Go out where?" asked his wife.
"To the Wide Water," said Hedgehog.

So they packed their picnic in a green rucksack, put their frog-dog on his leash, and put their beautiful summer hats on. Hedgehog had a panama hat, and Mrs Hedgehog had a hat with a veil.

“Not far now,” said Hedgehog. “Over there beyond the bushes—can you see?”
“Yes, I can see very well, thank you,” said his wife. “What’s over there, then?”
“The Wide Water,” said Hedgehog.

When they reached the Wide Water they went out on the lake in a boat. It lay there gently rocking.
It was a lovely fine day, with only one cloud in the sky.

At tea-time Hedgehog fried a fish, while Mrs Hedgehog splashed about in the water. "What a lovely day, dear," she told her husband. She was quite right, too.

All this time, however, Hare was limping on. He had limped a long, long way when he came to a milestone saying 145 MILES, and then he fell over.
He lay there, looking back the way he had come. He couldn't wait to tell Hedgehog that he, Hare, had won the race!
Because he felt sure he must have won it. Hare with his long legs.

But then it occurred to him that Hedgehog might have caught a train, and he might be coming down the road from the opposite direction. And he might say he got here first, ages ago, and he'd been waiting for Hare.
And he, Hedgehog, had won the race.
Then he fell asleep, no strength left and his leg broken. Someone took him to the animal hospital where he stayed for several days.
Nothing was ever heard of him any more.

But Hedgehog and his wife had had a little rest after their nice picnic, and when evening came they went home. They slept soundly until nine o'clock next morning. And as for Hare, why, Hedgehog never gave him another thought.

Now then, can anyone tell me who actually won that race?
Who was the winner?
The real winner, I mean?
With his short legs.
Yes, that's right! Perfectly correct.
It was H . . . . , with his . . . . . legs.

Translated by Anthea Bell

British Library Cataloguing in Publication Data

Janosch
The curious tale of hare and hedgehog.
Rn: Horst Eckert I. Title II. Der Wettlauf zwischen Hase und Igel. *English*
833′.914[J] PZ7

ISBN 0 86264 100 4